The Little
Bean
Cookbook

THE LITTLE

BEAN

— COOKBOOK —

ULTIMATE
EDITIONS

First published by Ultimate Editions in 1996

© 1996 Anness Publishing Limited

Ultimate Editions is an imprint of
Anness Publishing Limited
1 Boundary Row
London SE1 8HP

This edition distributed in Canada by
Book Express, an imprint of
Raincoast Books Distribution Limited

ISBN 1 86035 149 2

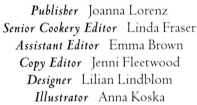

Publisher Joanna Lorenz
Senior Cookery Editor Linda Fraser
Assistant Editor Emma Brown
Copy Editor Jenni Fleetwood
Designer Lilian Lindblom
Illustrator Anna Koska
Photographers Karl Adamson, Michael Michaels, James Duncan, Steve
Baxter, Amanda Heywood, Patrick McLeavey, David Armstrong,
Michelle Garrett & Edward Allwright
Recipes Christine France, Roz Denny, Annie Nichols, Carla Capalbo,
Frances Cleary, Soheila Kimberley, Laura Washburn, Shehzad Husain,
Ruby Le Bois, Rosamund Grant, Liz Trigg, Alex Barker, Carole Clements,
Elizabeth Wolf-Cohen, Rafi Fernandez

For all recipes, quantities are given in both metric and imperial measures, and, where
appropriate, measures are also given in standard cups and spoons. Follow one set, but
not a mixture, because they are not interchangeable.

Printed in China

Contents

Introduction

Packed with protein, gentle on the pocket, convenient and easy to prepare, pulses are the perfect choice for today's cook. Dried beans and lentils are astonishingly versatile,  playing a starring role in starters, soups, salads, bakes and casseroles. Every nation has its own favourite recipes, from France's cassoulet to Mexico's chilli con carne. In China and Japan dried beans are even used to make confectionery.

The popularity of pulses dates from early in man's history. Esau's pottage was a bowl of lentils, and beans were used by the ancient Romans to cast votes: white beans signifying aye and coloured beans nay. During the feast of Saturnalia, a bean was used to decide who should preside over the festivities, a custom which survived in Britain in the baking of the Twelfth Night Cake. A dried bean and pea were baked in the cake, the finder of the bean being declared "Lord of Misrule", and she who found the pea being crowned Queen for the duration of the festivities.

In countries where large proportions of the population do not eat meat, such as India, pulses have always been a very important part of the national diet. The West has had a more ambivalent attitude: pulses were valued during the last war, but their popularity lessened once meat was more readily available.

The situation has reversed again during the last decade or so. Today, pulses are very definitely back on the menu, prized for being high in fibre and lower in fat than any other protein food. To make the most of pulse protein, it should be combined with a cereal (such as rice, pasta or bread), with nuts or seeds (especially sesame seeds or cashews), or dairy protein. These combinations occur naturally in recipes like Pasta and Dried Bean Soup, Bean and Nut Salad, Red Beans and Rice and even that old favourite, baked beans on toast.

In many of the recipes that follow, other types of bean may be substituted for those suggested. Don't be afraid to experiment: every bean has its own character and you may well find you prefer the earthy taste of red kidney beans or the subtle sweetness of aduki. When substituting one type of bean for another, check cooking times, however, as these vary considerably.

Buy dried beans and lentils from a market or shop with a rapid turnover, and store them in airtight containers. Use

within 9 months, before they start to shrivel and harden. All pulses, other than red split lentils and green mung beans, must be reconstituted by being soaked in water before cooking. Follow the cooking times suggested, checking frequently. Beans that are to be cooked again, in a soup or casserole perhaps, should be drained when they are just tender; beans intended for a purée should be soft but not mushy. The same goes for beans to be served in salads – because they will firm up on cooling, they need to be really tender.

Many types of dried bean are freely available in cans – they are ready-cooked, which is a great time saver for the busy cook. Take the trouble to get to know these, and the vast array of dried beans, and you'll discover a world of new cookery ideas.

Dried Beans & Pulses

ADUKI BEANS

Used for sprouting as well as serving as a vegetable, these are small reddish-brown beans with a sweet, nutty flavour. Cook soaked aduki beans for 30–35 minutes.

BLACK BEANS

These shiny black beans, related to kidney beans, are very popular in Caribbean and Chinese cookery. Cook soaked black beans for about 1 hour.

BLACK-EYED BEANS

Easily identified by the single black spot, these small beige beans (also known as black-eyed peas) have a savoury flavour. Cook the soaked beans for 30–45 minutes.

BORLOTTI BEANS

Attractive pinky-brown speckled beans, these cook to a creamy consistency and are used for dips and salads, as well as bakes. Cook the soaked beans for about 1 hour.

BUTTER BEANS

These flat white beans have to be cooked carefully, as they readily become mushy. They are very popular in salads, bakes and curries. Cook soaked butter beans for about 1–1¼ hours.

CANNELLINI BEANS

Small and white, these are related to kidney beans. Use them in place of haricot beans or butter beans. Cook soaked cannellini beans for about 1 hour, or until tender.

CHICK-PEAS

Ranging in colour from beige to golden brown, these beans (also called garbanzos) have a distinctive, slightly nutty flavour. They are delicious in dips (houmus), salads and curries. Cook soaked chick-peas for 1½–2 hours.

GREEN MUNG BEANS

Although best known for sprouting, green mung beans also make good eating. They cook quickly without soaking and are often puréed. Cook unsoaked mung beans for 30–35 minutes.

HARICOT BEANS

This family of oval-shaped beans comes in a range of sizes, from the pearl haricot to the large white bean. The popular canned baked beans are haricots. Soaked haricots should be cooked for 1–1½ hours.

LENTILS

It is important to distinguish between Continental (green or brown) lentils, which retain their shape after cooking, and split red lentils, which cook down to a golden purée. Cook soaked Continental lentils for 30–45 minutes; red lentils do not need soaking and cook in 20–25 minutes.

PINTO BEANS

Speckled or white, these medium-sized beans have a floury texture when cooked and are a popular ingredient of soups and casseroles. Cook soaked pinto beans for 1–1¼ hours, until tender.

RED KIDNEY BEANS

These delicious, distinctive beans are an essential ingredient of chilli con carne. Soaked dried red kidney beans must be boiled hard for 10 minutes at the start of cooking to eliminate natural toxins, then cooked for 1–1¼ hours, until tender.

SOYA BEANS

High in protein, these versatile beans can be boiled, but are also the source of soya milk, soya flour, tofu and soy sauce. The small hard beans need a long soak before being cooked for as long as 4 hours. Soya splits are partially cooked, do not need soaking, and cook in about half an hour.

Techniques

PICKING OVER

Modern packaging means that most pulses are free of foreign bodies, but it is still a good idea to spread them out and check for stones or twigs. Rinse in cold water and drain before soaking in a bowl.

SHORT SOAK

Tip the cleaned pulses into a saucepan, pour over cold water to cover and bring to the boil. Boil hard for 3–5 minutes, then remove the pan from the heat and leave to stand for 1 hour.

SOAKING

The only pulses that do not need to be soaked in water before they are cooked are split red lentils and green mung beans, although even these will cook more rapidly if soaked. Tip the pulses into a bowl and cover with cold water to twice their depth. Soak for 6–8 hours, or preferably overnight. Rinse the pulses well after soaking, as this helps to make them more digestible.

COOKING

Cook the drained pulses in 2–3 times their volume of water or unsalted stock. Bring the liquid to the boil, then lower the heat and simmer until tender (see pages 8–9 for timing). Add salt at the end of cooking; if added too soon salt will toughen the beans. Note: Red kidney beans must be boiled hard for 10 minutes before simmering. This will destroy any toxins present in the beans.

10

MICROWAVE COOKING

Pulses do not cook particularly well in the microwave, nor is there much to gain in terms of time. If you must cook beans and lentils this way, use a deep bowl, add plenty of boiling water and cook on High (100 per cent power) until tender. Check after two-thirds of the conventional cooking time. It is recommended that you do not cook red kidney beans by this method.

PRESSURE COOKING

You can save time by cooking soaked beans and lentils in the pressure cooker. Generally, timing should be about a third of that stated for conventional cooking; consult your handbook for more information.

SPROUTING BEANS

Nutritious beansprouts make a delicious addition to salads, sandwiches and stir-fries. To grow your own, you need a large, clean wide-mouthed jar, plus a circle of fine nylon gauze or cheesecloth for a cover. Spoon dried aduki beans, green mung beans or soya beans into the jar, filling it one-sixth full. Fit the cover, keeping it in place with an elastic band, then fill the jar with cold water. Drain well, then place the jar in a cool, dark place. Rinse and drain the beans daily. They will sprout in 2–3 days and will be ready to eat in less than a week.

11

COOK'S TIP

Buy beans for sprouting from health food shops to ensure that they are of good quality. Avoid using commercial seeds in case they have been treated with fungicides or pesticides.

Soups & Starters

Cauliflower, Flageolet & Fennel Seed Soup

INGREDIENTS

15ml/1 tbsp olive oil
1 garlic clove, crushed
1 onion, chopped
10ml/2 tsp fennel seeds
1 cauliflower, cut in small florets
2 x 400g/14oz cans flageolet beans,
drained and rinsed
1.1 litres/2 pints/5 cups vegetable stock
or water
salt and ground black pepper
chopped fresh parsley, to garnish
toasted slices of French bread,
to serve

SERVES 4–6

2 Bring to the boil. Reduce the heat and simmer for 10 minutes, or until the cauliflower is tender.

1 Heat the olive oil in a flameproof casserole. Add the garlic, onion and fennel seeds and cook for 5 minutes or until the onion softens. Add the cauliflower florets, half of the flageolet beans and the vegetable stock or water. Stir gently until well mixed.

3 Pureé the soup in a blender or food processor and return it to the pan. Stir in the remaining beans and season to taste. Reheat the soup and pour into heated bowls.

Sprinkle with chopped parsley and serve the soup at once, with toasted slices of French bread.

Bean Nachos

INGREDIENTS

30ml/2 tbsp corn oil
2 onions, chopped
2 garlic cloves, chopped
3 jalapeño peppers, seeded and chopped
25ml/1½ tbsp mild chilli powder
450g/16oz can red kidney beans, drained and liquid reserved
45ml/3 tbsp chopped fresh coriander
1 large packet round tortilla chips
225g/8oz/2 cups grated Cheddar cheese
50g/2oz/½ cup pitted black olives, thinly sliced
fresh coriander sprigs, for garnishing (optional)

SERVES 8

1 Preheat the oven to 220°C/425°F/Gas 7.

2 Heat the oil in a frying pan. Add the onions, garlic and jalapeños and cook for about 5 minutes, until soft. Add the chilli powder and cook for 1 minute more.

3 Stir the beans into the onion mixture, then stir in 120ml/4fl oz/½ cup of reserved liquid from the beans. Cook for about 10 minutes, until thick, mashing the beans with a fork from time to time. Remove the pan from the heat and stir in the chopped fresh coriander.

4 Put a little of the bean mixture on each tortilla chip. Top each nacho with a little cheese and a slice of olive. Arrange the topped chips on a baking sheet.

5 Bake for 5–10 minutes, until the cheese has all melted and is beginning to brown. Serve at once, garnished with coriander, if you like.

Falafel

INGREDIENTS

450g / 1 lb / 2 cups dried white beans
2 red onions, chopped
2 large garlic cloves, crushed
45ml / 3 tbsp finely chopped fresh parsley
5ml / 1 tsp ground coriander
5ml / 1 tsp ground cumin
7.5ml / 1½ tsp baking powder
oil, for deep frying
salt and ground black pepper
tomato salad, to serve

SERVES 6

I Soak the white beans overnight in water. Remove the skins and process in a blender or food processor. Add the chopped onions, the garlic, parsley, coriander,

cumin, baking powder and seasoning, and blend again to make a smooth paste. Cover the mixture and set it aside to stand at room temperature for at least 30 minutes to firm up.

2 Flatten walnut-size pieces of the mixture to make small patties. Fry them in batches in very hot oil until golden, then drain. Serve hot, with a tomato salad.

COOK'S TIP
Falafel are usually made with chick-peas. For this version, use haricot beans or butter beans.

20

Bean & Nut Salad

INGREDIENTS

75g / 3oz / scant ½ cup red kidney, pinto or
borlotti beans
75g / 3oz / scant ½ cup white cannellini or
butter beans
30ml / 2 tbsp olive oil
175g / 6oz / 1 cup French beans, cut in
short lengths
3 spring onions, sliced
1 small yellow or red pepper, sliced
1 carrot, coarsely grated
30ml / 2 tbsp dried topping onions or sun-dried
tomatoes, chopped
50g / 2oz / ½ cup unsalted cashew nuts or
split almonds

DRESSING
45ml / 3 tbsp sunflower oil
30ml / 2 tbsp red wine vinegar
15ml / 1 tbsp coarse-grain mustard
5ml / 1 tsp caster sugar
5ml / 1 tsp dried mixed herbs
salt and ground black pepper

SERVES 6

1 Soak the beans, overnight if possible, then drain and rinse well, cover generously with cold water and cook according to the instructions on the packets.

2 When cooked, drain and season the beans and toss them in the olive oil in a large serving bowl. Leave to cool for 30 minutes.

3 Add all of the other vegetables, including the sun-dried tomatoes, but not the dried topping onions, if using. Stir in half the nuts and toss to mix. Make the dressing by shaking the ingredients together in a screw topped jar. Toss with the salad and serve sprinkled with the topping onions, if using, and the remaining nuts.

Warm Salad of Black-eyed Beans

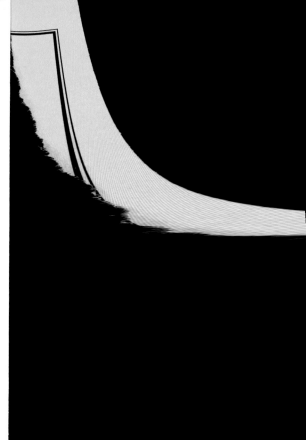

INGREDIENTS

250g/9oz/1½ cups black-eyed beans
1 bay leaf
2 small red peppers
2.5ml/½ tsp Dijon-style mustard
30ml/2 tbsp wine vinegar
1.5ml/¼ tsp salt
4ml/¾ tsp ground black pepper
90ml/6 tbsp olive oil
30ml/2 tbsp snipped fresh chives
8 rindless lean bacon rashers
flat leaf parsley, to garnish

SERVES 4

1 Soak the beans, overnight if possible, then drain and rinse well. Cover the beans generously with cold water, add the bay leaf, and cook for about 30–45 minutes, until tender.

2 Preheat the grill. Grill the peppers until charred on all sides, then steam them in a plastic bag for 10 minutes. Rub off all the skin. Cut the peppers in half,  discard the seeds, white membranes and stem, and slice into 1 x 5cm/½ x 2in strips.

3 Combine the mustard and vinegar in a small bowl. Add the salt and pepper. Beat in the oil until well blended. Add the chives.

4 Cook the bacon until crisp. Drain on kitchen paper. Cut or break the bacon into small pieces, set aside and keep warm.

5 When the beans are tender, drain them and discard the bay leaf. While they are still warm, toss them with the chive dressing. Mound the beans on a serving dish. Sprinkle with the warm bacon pieces and garnish with the strips of red pepper and a sprig of parsley. Serve the salad warm.

Pinto Bean Salad

INGREDIENTS

250g / 9oz / 1½ cups dried pinto beans, soaked
overnight and drained
1 bay leaf
45ml / 3 tbsp coarse salt
2 ripe tomatoes, diced
4 spring onions, finely chopped
fresh coriander or parsley, to garnish
DRESSING
50ml / 2fl oz / ¼ cup fresh lemon juice
5ml / 1 tsp salt
90ml / 6 tbsp olive oil
1 garlic clove, crushed
45ml / 3 tbsp chopped fresh coriander
ground black pepper

SERVES 4

I Put the beans in a large pan. Add cold water to cover and the bay leaf. Bring to the boil. Cover, and simmer for 30 minutes. Add the coarse salt and continue simmering for about 30 minutes more, until tender. Drain and let cool slightly. Discard the bay leaf.

2 Make the dressing. Mix the lemon juice with the salt with a fork, stirring until dissolved. Gradually stir in the oil until thick. Add the garlic, coriander, and pepper to taste.

3 While the beans are still warm, place them in a large bowl. Add the dressing and toss to coat. Let the beans cool completely. Add the tomatoes, reserving a little for garnish, and spring onions, and toss to mix evenly. Set aside for at least 30 minutes before serving, garnished with the reserved tomato and fresh coriander or parsley.

25

Tarka Dhal

INGREDIENTS

*115g/4oz/½ cup masoor dhal (split
red lentils)*
*50g/2oz/¼ cup moong dhal (small split
yellow lentils)*
600ml/1 pint/2½ cups water
7ml/1 tsp finely grated fresh root ginger
5ml/1 tsp crushed garlic
1.5ml/¼ tsp turmeric
2 fresh green chillies, chopped
7.5ml/1½ tsp salt
TARKA
30ml/2 tbsp vegetable oil
1 onion, sliced
1.5ml/¼ tsp mixed mustard and onion seeds
4 dried red chillies
1 tomato, sliced
GARNISH
*15ml/1 tbsp chopped fresh coriander, plus
coriander sprig*
1-2 fresh green chillies, sliced
15ml/1 tbsp chopped fresh mint

SERVES 4

1 Pick over the lentils for any stones before washing them and draining them well. Pour the water into a saucepan and bring to the boil.

2 Add the lentils to the water, with the root ginger, garlic, turmeric and chopped green chillies. Cook for 15–20 minutes, or until soft. Stir occasionally.

3 Mash the lentil mixture to the consistency of a creamy chicken soup. If the dhal mixture looks too dry, stir in more water. Season with the salt.

4 Make the tarka. Heat the oil and fry the onion with the mustard and onion seeds, dried red chillies and sliced tomato for 2 minutes.

5 Pour the tarka over the dhal and garnish with fresh coriander, green chillies and mint.

COOK'S TIP
Dried red chillies are available in many different sizes. If the ones you have are large, or if you want a less spicy flavour, reduce the quantity specified to 1–2.

Tuscan Baked Beans

INGREDIENTS

*475g/18oz/3 cups dried beans, such as
cannellini
60ml/4 tbsp olive oil
2 garlic cloves, crushed
3 fresh sage leaves (if not available use
60ml/4 tbsp chopped fresh parsley)
1 leek, finely sliced
400g/14oz can plum tomatoes, chopped, with
their juice
salt and ground black pepper*

SERVES 6–8

28

1 Carefully pick over the beans, discarding any stones or other particles. Place the beans in a large bowl and cover with cold water. Soak for at least 6 hours, or overnight. Drain in a colander.

2 Preheat the oven to 180°C/350°F/Gas 4. In a small saucepan, heat the oil and sauté the garlic and fresh sage leaves for 3–4 minutes. Remove from the heat and set the pan aside.

3 In a flameproof casserole combine the drained beans with the leek and tomatoes. Stir in the oil with the garlic and sage. Add enough fresh water to cover the  beans by 2.5cm/1in. Mix well. Cover the casserole with a lid or foil, and place in the centre of the hot oven. Bake for 1¾ hours.

4 Remove the casserole from the oven, stir the beans, and season with salt and pepper. Return them to the oven, uncovered, and cook for another 15 minutes, or until the beans are tender and drying out a little on top to form a crust. Remove from the oven and allow to stand for at least 7–8 minutes before serving. This dish is excellent served either hot or at room temperature.

Stewed Lentils

INGREDIENTS

450g / 1lb / 2 cups green or brown lentils
45ml / 3 tbsp olive oil
50g / 2oz / ¼ cup pancetta or salt pork
1 onion, very finely chopped
1 celery stick, very finely sliced
1 carrot, very finely chopped
1 clove garlic, peeled
1 bay leaf
45ml / 3 tbsp chopped fresh parsley
salt and ground black pepper

SERVES 6

2 Add the celery and carrot and cook for 3–4 minutes more, stirring occasionally.

I Carefully pick over the lentils, removing small stones or other particles. Place the lentils in a large bowl and cover with water. Soak for several hours. Drain. In a large, heavy saucepan heat the oil. Add the pancetta or salt pork and cook gently for 3–4 minutes. Stir in the onion, and cook over a low heat until it is soft, stirring the mixture frequently.

3 Add the lentils to the pan, stirring to coat them with the fat. Pour in enough boiling water just to cover the lentils. Stir well, adding the whole garlic clove,  the bay leaf and the parsley. Season with salt and pepper. Cook over a medium heat for about I hour, until the lentils are tender. Discard the garlic and bay leaf. Serve hot or at room temperature.

Red Beans & Rice

INGREDIENTS

3 cups dried red kidney beans,
soaked overnight
2 bay leaves
2 tablespoons oil or bacon grease
1 onion, chopped
2 garlic cloves, finely chopped
2 stalks celery, sliced
8 ounces salt pork or uncooked ham
2¼ cups long-grain rice
3 tablespoons chopped fresh parsley
salt and freshly ground black pepper

SERVES 8–10

1 Drain the beans and put them into a large pan with fresh cold water to cover generously. Bring to a boil and boil rapidly for 10 minutes, then drain and rinse both the beans and the pan.

2 Return the beans to the pan with the bay leaves and fresh cold water to cover. Bring to a boil, then simmer for about 30 minutes. Add more water as needed.

3 Heat the oil in a frying pan. Cook the onion, garlic, and celery until soft. Stir the mixture into the beans and push the salt pork or ham into the middle.

4 Simmer, adding water as necessary, for another 45 minutes or so, until the beans are very tender. Add salt, if necessary, 15–20 minutes before the end of the cooking time.

5 Put the rice into a saucepan and add 1½ times its volume of cold water, plus 1 teaspoon salt. Bring to a boil, stirring occasionally. Cover the pan tightly and leave over very low heat for 12 minutes. Without lifting the lid, turn off the heat and leave the rice undisturbed for another 12 minutes (the rice should be cooked and all the liquid absorbed).

6 Remove the meat from the beans and dice it, removing the fat and rind. Drain the beans and add the diced pork. Season to taste.

7 Fluff the rice with a fork (if the rice has not absorbed all the liquid, drain the excess), stir in the parsley, then serve on a warmed platter, topped with the red beans.

Vegetarian Dishes

Potato-topped Lentil Pie

INGREDIENTS

1kg / 2¼lb potatoes
45ml / 3 tbsp extra virgin olive oil
1 large onion, chopped
1 green pepper, chopped
2 carrots, coarsely grated
2 garlic cloves
40g / 1½oz / 3 tbsp butter
200g / 7oz / 1¼ cups mushrooms, chopped
2 x 400g / 14oz cans aduki beans, drained
600ml / 1 pint / 2½ cups stock
5ml / 1 tsp yeast extract
2 bay leaves
5ml / 1 tsp dried mixed herbs
salt and ground black pepper
dried breadcrumbs or chopped nuts, to sprinkle

SERVES 6–8

2 Stir in the mushrooms and beans and cook for a further 2 minutes, then add the stock, yeast extract, bay leaves and mixed herbs. Simmer for 15 minutes, stirring often. Preheat the grill. Remove the bay leaves and tip the vegetable mixture into a shallow ovenproof dish. Spoon the mashed potato on top, spread it roughly, and sprinkle over the crumbs or nuts. Grill until golden brown.

1 Boil the potatoes until tender, then drain, peel and mash with the oil. Season. Fry the onion, pepper, carrots and garlic in the butter, until they are tender.

> ### COOK'S TIP
> Potatoes are easier to peel when boiled in their skins; this also preserves vitamins.

33

Turnip & Chick-pea Cobbler

INGREDIENTS

45ml/3 tbsp sunflower oil
1 onion, sliced
2 carrots, chopped
3 medium turnips, chopped
1 small sweet potato or swede, chopped
2 celery sticks, thinly sliced
2.5ml/½ tsp ground coriander
2.5ml/½ tsp dried mixed herbs
425g/15oz can chopped tomatoes
400g/14oz can chick-peas
1 vegetable stock cube
salt and ground black pepper
green leafy vegetables, to serve
TOPPING
225g/8oz/2 cups self-raising flour
5ml/1 tsp baking powder
50g/2oz/4 tbsp margarine
45ml/3 tbsp sunflower seeds
30ml/2 tbsp grated Parmesan cheese
150ml/¼ pint/⅔ cup milk, plus extra
for brushing

SERVES 4–6

1 Heat the oil and fry the vegetables for about 10 minutes until they are soft. Add the coriander, herbs, tomatoes, chick-peas with the can liquid and stock cube. Season well and simmer for 20 minutes. Pour the vegetables into a shallow casserole while you make the cobbler topping. Preheat the oven to 190°C/375°F/Gas 5.

2 Mix the flour with the baking powder, then rub in the margarine until the mixture resembles bread-crumbs. Stir in the sunflower seeds and the cheese. Add the milk and mix to a firm dough. Lightly roll out the topping to a thickness of 1cm/½in and stamp out star shapes or rounds, or simply cut it into small squares.

3 Place the shapes on top of the vegetable mixture and brush with a little extra milk. Bake for about 12–15 minutes until well risen and golden brown. Serve hot with green, leafy vegetables.

Aduki Bean Burgers

INGREDIENTS

*200g / 7oz / 1 cup brown rice
(not quick-cook variety)
1 onion, chopped
2 garlic cloves, crushed
30ml / 2 tbsp sunflower oil
50g / 2oz / 4 tbsp butter
1 small green pepper, seeded and chopped
1 carrot, coarsely grated
400g / 14oz can aduki beans, drained
(or 115g / 4oz / ⅔ cup dried aduki beans, soaked
and cooked)
1 egg, beaten
115g / 4oz / 1 cup grated mature Cheddar cheese
5ml / 1 tsp dried thyme
50g / 2oz / ½ cup roasted hazelnuts or toasted
flaked almonds
salt and ground black pepper
wholemeal flour or cornmeal, for coating
oil, for frying
buns, salad and relish, to serve*

SERVES 12

1 Cook the rice according to the instructions on the packet, allowing it to slightly overcook so that it is soft. Drain the rice and transfer it to a large bowl. Fry the onion and garlic in the oil and butter, together with the green pepper and carrot, for about 10 minutes, until the vegetables are softened.

2 Mix this vegetable mixture into the rice, together with the aduki beans, egg, cheese, thyme and nuts. Add plenty of seasoning. Chill until quite firm.

3 Shape into 12 patties, using wet hands if the mixture sticks. Coat the patties in flour or cornmeal and set aside. Heat 1cm / ½in oil in a large, shallow pan  and fry the aduki burgers in batches until browned on each side, about 5 minutes in total. Remove and drain on kitchen paper. Serve in buns with salad and relish. Freeze any left-over burgers.

COOK'S TIP

To freeze the burgers, cool them after cooking, then open freeze them before wrapping and bagging. Use within 6 weeks. Cook from frozen by baking in a preheated moderately-hot oven for 20–25 minutes.

Red Bean Chilli

INGREDIENTS

30ml/2 tbsp vegetable oil
1 onion, chopped
400g/14oz can chopped tomatoes
2 garlic cloves, crushed
300ml/½ pint/1¼ cups white wine
about 300ml/½ pint/1¼ cups vegetable stock
2 thyme sprigs or 5ml/1 tsp dried thyme
10ml/2 tsp ground cumin
115g/4oz/½ cup red lentils
45ml/3 tbsp dark soy sauce
½ red chilli, finely chopped
5ml/1 tsp mixed spice
225g/8oz can red kidney beans, drained
10ml/2 tsp sugar
salt
boiled rice and sweetcorn, to serve

SERVES 4

2 Stir in the soy sauce, chilli and mixed spice. Cover and simmer for 40 minutes, or until the lentils are cooked, stirring occasionally and adding more water if the lentils begin to dry out.

3 Stir in the kidney beans and continue cooking for 10 minutes, adding a little extra stock or water if necessary. Season with the sugar and salt to taste. Serve hot, with boiled rice and sweetcorn.

I Heat the oil and fry the onion until soft. Stir in the tomatoes and the garlic. Cook for 10 minutes, then stir in the wine and the stock, thyme, cumin and lentils.

38

Kenyan Mung Bean Stew

INGREDIENTS

*225g / 8oz / 1¼ cups mung beans, soaked
overnight and drained
25g / 1oz / 2 tbsp butter
1 red onion, chopped
2 garlic cloves, crushed
30ml / 2 tbsp tomato purée
½ green pepper, seeded and cut in small cubes
½ red pepper, seeded and cut in small cubes
1 green chilli, seeded and finely chopped
300ml / ½ pint / 1¼ cups water*

SERVES 4

39

1 Cook the mung beans, in water to cover, until soft and the water has evaporated. Mash roughly and set aside. Heat the butter and fry the onion and garlic until golden, then stir in the tomato purée and cook for a further 2–3 minutes, stirring. Add the mashed beans with the peppers and chilli.

2 Add the water, a little at a time, stirring well to mix all the ingredients together.

3 Pour back into a clean saucepan and simmer for about 10 minutes, then check the seasoning, spoon into a serving dish, and serve at once.

COOK'S TIP

If you prefer a more traditional, smoother texture, cook the mung beans until very soft, then mash them thoroughly until smooth.

Black-eyed Bean Stew with Spicy Pumpkin

INGREDIENTS

225g/ 8oz/ 1¼ cups black-eyed beans, soaked
for 4 hours or overnight
1 onion, chopped
1 green or red pepper, seeded
and chopped
2 garlic cloves, chopped
1 vegetable stock cube
2 thyme sprigs or 5ml/ 1 tsp dried thyme
5ml/ 1 tsp paprika
2.5ml/ ½ tsp mixed spice
Tabasco sauce
2 carrots, sliced
15-30ml/ 1-2 tbsp sunflower oil
salt and ground black pepper
thyme sprigs, to garnish
SPICY PUMPKIN
25g/ 1oz/ 2 tbsp butter
or margarine
675g/ 1½lb pumpkin, cut in cubes
3 tomatoes, peeled and chopped
1 onion, finely chopped
2 garlic cloves, crushed
2.5ml/ ½ tsp ground cinnamon
10ml/ 2 tsp curry powder
pinch of grated nutmeg
300ml/ ½ pint/ 1¼ cups water
Tabasco sauce

SERVES 3–4

40

1 Drain the beans, place in a pan and cover generously with water. Bring the beans to the boil. Add the onion, green or red pepper, garlic, stock cube, thyme and spices. Simmer for 45 minutes, or until the beans are just tender. Season to taste with salt and a little Tabasco sauce.

2 Add the carrots and oil and continue cooking for about 10–12 minutes, until the carrots are cooked, adding a little more water, if necessary. Remove from direct heat but keep hot until required.

3 Make the spicy pumpkin. Melt the butter or margarine in a big frying pan or saucepan, and add all the pumpkin, tomatoes, onion, garlic, spices and water. Stir well to combine and simmer until the pumpkin is soft. Season with Tabasco sauce, salt and black pepper, to taste. Serve with the black-eyed beans. Garnish the dish with thyme.

Bean & Barley Bowl

INGREDIENTS

45ml/3 tbsp sunflower oil
1 red onion, sliced
½ fennel bulb, sliced
2 carrots, cut in sticks
1 parsnip, sliced
115g/4oz/1 cup pearl barley
1 litre/1¾ pints/4 cups stock
5ml/1 tsp dried thyme
115g/4oz/⅔ cup green beans, sliced
425g/15oz can pinto beans, drained
salt and ground black pepper
chopped fresh parsley, to garnish
cheese croûtes, to serve (see Cook's Tip)

SERVES 6

1 Heat the oil in a flameproof casserole. Sauté the onion, the fennel, carrot sticks and parsnip slices for 10 minutes. Stir in the barley and stock. Bring to the boil, add the thyme and seasoning, then cover and simmer gently for 40 minutes.

2 Stir in the sliced green beans and drained pinto beans. Cover the casserole and continue cooking for a further 20 minutes.

3 Ladle the bean stew into heated bowls, sprinkle with parsley, and serve, accompanied by cheese croûtes, if liked.

COOK'S TIP

To make cheese croûtes: slice a baguette, brush the slices with oil and place them on a baking sheet. Bake at 190°C/375°F/Gas 5 for about 15 minutes, until light golden. Quickly rub each croûte with the cut halves of 2 garlic cloves. Sprinkle over 60ml/4 tbsp grated Parmesan and return to the oven to melt the cheese.

Butter Bean & Pesto Pasta

INGREDIENTS

225g/8oz/2 cups pasta shapes
grated nutmeg
30ml/2 tbsp extra virgin olive oil
400g/14oz can butter beans, drained
45ml/3 tbsp pesto sauce
150ml/¼ pint/⅔ cup single cream
salt and ground black pepper
45ml/3 tbsp pine nuts and sprigs of fresh
basil, to garnish
grated cheese, to serve (optional)

SERVES 4

1 Boil the pasta until cooked but firm (*al dente*), then drain, leaving it a little moist. Return the pasta to the pan, season, and then stir in the nutmeg and oil.

2 Heat the beans in a saucepan with the pesto and the cream, stirring it until it begins to simmer. Toss all the bean and pesto sauce into the pasta and mix well.

3 Serve in bowls, garnished with the pine nuts and basil sprigs. Serve with grated cheese, if you like.

Fish &
Shellfish Dishes

Tuscan Tuna & Beans

INGREDIENTS

30ml/2 tbsp smooth French mustard
300ml/½ pint/1¼ cups olive oil
60ml/4 tbsp white wine vinegar
*30ml/2 tbsp chopped fresh parsley, plus extra
to garnish*
*30ml/2 tbsp snipped fresh chives, plus whole
chives to garnish*
*30ml/2 tbsp chopped fresh tarragon or chervil,
plus extra sprigs to garnish*
400g/14oz can haricot beans
400g/14oz can red kidney beans
1 red onion, finely chopped
*225g/8oz canned tuna in oil, drained and
lightly flaked*
sliced ciabatta, to serve

SERVES 4

1 In a small bowl, beat the mustard, oil, vinegar, parsley, chives and tarragon or chervil together.

2 Drain all the canned beans. Mix the chopped red onion, beans and tuna together in a bowl. Pour the dressing over the top and toss to mix. Transfer to a large serving dish or individual bowls and garnish with the whole chives and fresh herbs. Serve at once, with slices of fresh ciabatta.

Roast Cod with Mixed Beans

INGREDIENTS

4 thick cod steaks
45ml/3 tbsp sweet sherry or Madeira
400g/14oz can spicy mixed beans, drained
400g/14oz can kidney, borlotti or flageolet
beans, drained
2 garlic cloves, crushed
15ml/1 tbsp olive oil
5ml/1 tsp grated orange rind
15ml/1 tbsp chopped fresh parsley
salt and ground black pepper
strips of blanched orange rind and parsley
sprigs, to garnish

SERVES 4–6

2 Preheat the oven to 200°C/ 400°F/ Gas 6. Mix the beans with the garlic and place in the base of an ovenproof dish. Place the fish on top and pour over the sherry or Madeira. Brush the fish with the oil, then sprinkle with the orange rind, half the parsley and salt and pepper to taste.

3 Cover tightly with foil. Cook for 15–20 minutes. Pierce the thickest part of the fish with a knife to check if it is cooked through and continue cooking for only another 2–3 minutes, if necessary.

4 Baste the fish with a little of the juices which have risen up to the top of the beans during cooking. Serve the fish and beans at once, on heated plates. Sprinkle with the rest of the parsley just before serving and garnish each portion with a few strips of pared orange rind, blanched in boiling water for a couple of minutes, and a sprig of fresh parsley.

1 Skin the thick cod steaks and place them in a shallow dish. Pour over all the sherry or Madeira and marinate for 10 minutes. Turn the steaks once.

Haddock with Lentils & Leeks

INGREDIENTS

150g / 5oz / ⅔ cup green lentils
1 bay leaf
1 garlic clove, finely chopped
grated rind of 1 orange
grated rind of 1 lemon
pinch of ground cumin
15g / ½oz / 1 tbsp butter
450g / 1lb leeks, thinly sliced or cut in
julienne strips
300ml / ½ pint / 1¼ cups whipping cream
15ml / 1 tbsp lemon juice, or to taste
800g / 1¾lb thick skinless haddock
or cod fillet
salt and ground black pepper

SERVES 4

48

1 Rinse the lentils and put them in a large saucepan with the bay leaf and garlic. Add enough water to cover by 5cm/2in. Bring to the boil, and boil gently for 10 minutes, then reduce the heat and simmer for a further 15–30 minutes, until the lentils are just tender and almost dry.

2 Drain the lentils and discard the bay leaf, then stir in half the orange rind and all the lemon rind, and season well with ground cumin and salt and pepper.

Transfer to a shallow baking dish or gratin dish. Preheat the oven to 190°C/375°F/Gas 5.

3 Melt the butter in a saucepan over a medium heat, then add the leeks and cook, stirring frequently, until softened. Add 225ml/8fl oz/1 cup of the cream and the remaining orange rind and cook gently for 15–20 minutes, until all the leeks are completely soft and the cream has begun to thicken. Stir in the lemon juice and season with salt and plenty of pepper.

4 Cut the fish into four pieces. With your fingertips, locate and pull out any small bones. Season the fish with salt and pepper, place it on top of the lentil mixture and press down slightly into the lentils. Cover each piece of fish with a quarter of the leek mixture and pour 15ml/1 tbsp of the remaining cream over each piece. Bake for 30 minutes until the fish is cooked through and the topping is lightly golden. Serve the dish at once; it needs no extra accompaniment.

Clam & Sausage Chilli

INGREDIENTS

175g/6oz/1 cup dried black beans, soaked
overnight and drained
1 bay leaf
5ml/1 tsp coarse salt
225g/8oz lean sausagemeat
15ml/1 tbsp vegetable oil
1 onion, very finely chopped
1 garlic clove, crushed
5ml/1 tsp fennel seeds
5ml/1 tsp dried oregano
1.5ml/¼ tsp red pepper flakes, or to taste
10-15ml/2-3 tsp chilli powder, or to taste
5ml/1 tsp ground cumin
2 x 450g/16oz cans chopped tomatoes in
tomato juice
120ml/4fl oz/½ cup dry white wine
2 x 275g/10oz cans clams, drained and
liquid reserved
salt and ground black pepper
French or soda bread, to serve (optional)

SERVES 4

1 Put the beans in a large pan. Add fresh cold water to cover and the bay leaf. Bring to the boil, then cover, and simmer for 30 minutes. Add the coarse salt and continue simmering for about 30 minutes more, until tender. Drain and discard the bay leaf.

2 Put the sausagemeat in a flameproof casserole and cook over a medium heat, for 2–3 minutes, until just beginning to brown. Stir frequently to break up lumps. Add the oil, onion, and garlic.

3 Continue cooking for about 5 minutes more, until the vegetables are soft, stirring occasionally.

4 Stir in the herbs, spices, tomatoes, wine and 150ml/ ¼ pint/¾ cup of the reserved clam juice. Bring to the boil, then lower the heat and cook, stirring occasion-ally, for about 15 minutes, or until the sauce is thick and full of flavour.

5 Add the black beans and clams and stir to mix. Continue cooking just until the clams are heated through. Adjust the seasoning, if necessary. Serve immediately, with slices of French bread or chunks of home-made soda bread, if you like.

50

Roast Leg of Lamb with Beans

INGREDIENTS

2.75-3kg/6-7lb leg of lamb
3 or 4 garlic cloves
olive oil
fresh rosemary leaves
450g/1lb/2½ cups dried haricot or flageolet
beans, soaked overnight in cold water
1 bay leaf
30ml/2 tbsp red wine
150ml/¼ pint/⅔ cup lamb or beef stock
30g/1oz/2 tbsp butter
salt and ground black pepper
watercress, to garnish

SERVES 8–10

I First, preheat the oven to 220°C/ 425°F/ Gas 7. Wipe the leg of lamb with damp kitchen paper and dry the fat covering well. Cut 2 or 3 of the garlic cloves into 10–12 slivers, then with the tip of a knife, cut 10–12 slits into the lamb and insert the garlic slivers into the slits. Rub with oil, season with salt and pepper and sprinkle with rosemary.

2 Set the lamb on a rack in a shallow roasting tin and cook for 15 minutes. Reduce the heat to 180°C/ 350°F/ Gas 4 and continue to roast for 1½–1¾ hours (about 18 minutes per 450g/1lb). Baste the lamb from time to time.

3 Meanwhile, rinse the beans and put in a saucepan with enough fresh water to cover generously. Add the remaining garlic and the bay leaf, then bring to the boil. Reduce the heat and simmer for 45–60 minutes, until the beans are tender, stirring occasionally and adding more water if needed.

4 Transfer the lamb to a board and leave to stand, loosely covered, for 10–15 minutes. Skim off the fat from the cooking juices, then add the wine and stock to the roasting tin. Boil over a medium heat, stirring and scraping the base of the tin, until slightly reduced. Strain into a warmed gravy boat.

5 Drain the beans, discard the bay leaf, then toss the beans with the butter until it melts. Season with salt and pepper. Serve the lamb on a platter with the beans and garnish with watercress. Offer the rich red wine gravy separately.

Hot and Sour Meat & Lentil Curry

INGREDIENTS

60ml/ 4 tbsp vegetable oil
5 green chillies, seeded and chopped
30ml/ 2 tbsp grated fresh root ginger
3 garlic cloves, crushed
2 bay leaves
5cm/ 2in cinnamon stick
900g/ 2lb lean lamb, cut in large pieces
115g/ 4oz/ ⅔ cup yellow split peas
115g/ 4oz/ ⅔ cup red lentils
2 potatoes, cubed and soaked in water
1 aubergine, cubed and soaked in water
3 sliced onions, deep-fried and drained
50g/ 2oz frozen spinach, thawed and drained
25g/ 1oz fresh or dried fenugreek leaves
2 carrots
50g/ 2oz/ 2 cups chopped fresh mint leaves
115g/ 4oz/ 4 cups chopped fresh coriander
20ml/ 4 tsp garam masala
7.5ml/ 1½ tsp star anise powder
3.75ml/ ¾ tsp ground nutmeg
7.5ml/ 1½ tsp fenugreek powder
5ml/ 1 tsp mustard powder
10ml/ 2 tsp red chilli powder
10ml/ 2 tsp brown sugar
60ml/ 4 tbsp tamarind juice
salt and ground black pepper
fried, sliced garlic, to garnish

SERVES 4–6

1 Heat half the oil and fry the chillies, ginger and garlic for 2 minutes. Add the bay leaves, cinnamon, lamb and 600ml/ 1 pint/ 2½ cups water. Simmer until the lamb is half cooked, then lift it out. Add the pulses to the pan and cook until tender. Mash roughly with the back of a spoon.

2 Drain the potatoes and aubergine and add to the pulse mix with the deep-fried onions, the spinach, fenugreek and carrots. Add some hot water if the mixture is too thick. Cook until the vegetables are tender, then mash again, keeping the vegetables a little coarse.

3 Heat the remaining oil and gently fry the mint leaves and coriander with the spices, sugar, salt and 5ml/ 1 tsp black pepper. Add the lamb and fry gently for 5 minutes. Return the spiced lamb to the lentil and vegetable mixture and stir well. Add liquid if necessary. Heat gently until the lamb is fully cooked.

4 Add the tamarind juice to the lamb mixture. Spoon into a serving dish and garnish with the fried garlic slices. Serve at once.

58

Lamb with Black-eyed Peas & Pumpkin

INGREDIENTS

1 pound lean boneless lamb, cubed
4 cups chicken or lamb broth or water
½ cup black-eyed peas, soaked for
6 hours or overnight, drained
1 onion, chopped
2 garlic cloves, crushed
2½ tablespoons tomato paste
1½ teaspoons dried thyme
1½ teaspoons vegetable oil
1 teaspoon pumpkin pie spice
½ teaspoon freshly ground black pepper
¾ cup pumpkin, chopped
Tabasco sauce
salt
boiled yam, plantain or sweet potatoes,
to serve (optional)

SERVES 4

1 Put the lamb in a large saucepan with the broth and bring to a boil, skimming off any foam, then reduce the heat, cover and simmer for 1 hour.

2 Stir in the black-eyed peas and continue cooking for about 35 minutes.

3 Add the onion, garlic, tomato paste, thyme, oil, pumpkin pie spice, black pepper, salt and Tabasco sauce and cook for 15 more minutes or until all the beans are tender.  Add the pumpkin and simmer for about 10 minutes, until the pumpkin is very soft and almost mushy. Serve with boiled yam, plantains or sweet potatoes, if you like.

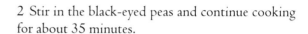

COOK'S TIP

Any dried white beans can be used instead of black-eyed peas. If you prefer a firmer texture, cook the pumpkin for just 5 minutes, until barely tender.

60

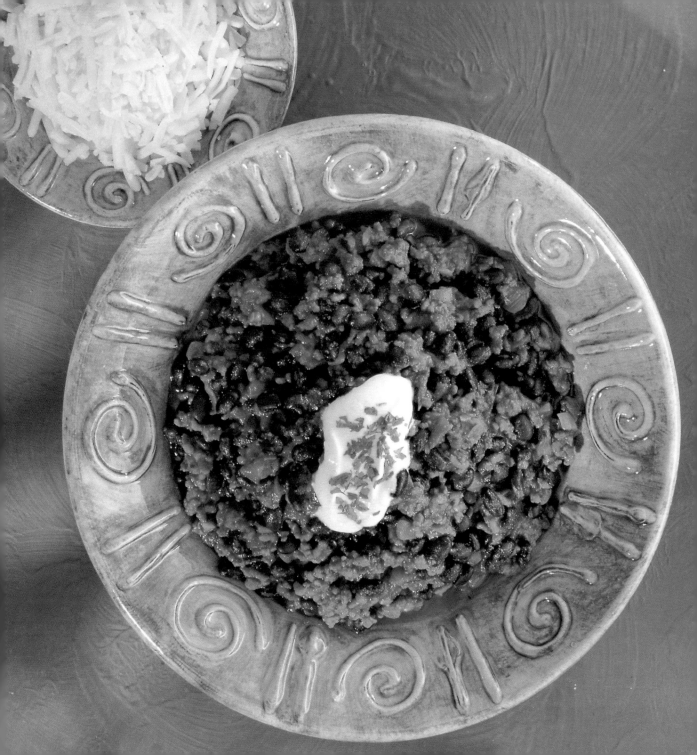

Index